The Edge of a Cry
Kʌ pəmp ka ʌrɔŋ

Oumar Farouk Sesay

Sierra Leonean Writers Series

The Edge of a Cry
Kʌ pəmp ka ʌrɔŋ

ISBN: 978-99910-54-06-3

Sierra Leonean Writers Series
Warima / Freetown / Accra
120 Kissy Road, Freetown, Sierra Leone
Publisher: Osman Sankoh (Mallam O.)
www.sl-writers-series.org
publisher@sl-writers-series.org

CONTENTS

Dedicated to my daughters:

Oumou Kultum
Rugiatu Tudadu

Commentary

The title of this volume is, in many ways, a misleading one, as what is offered is vastly more than a cry by a poet consumed with issues of such deep resonance for all of us, that we soon forget the marginal Cry. If his pivot is the wounded knee of his homeland, Oumar Farouk Sesay's poems not only heal that iconic image of Sierra Leone, they transform, in his searing consciousness and humanity, the land and its people, into a poetic affirmation of pride, resilience and hope. But there is more: we are invited to walk on the many roads that this poet has travelled, and see the complexities of other landscapes, listen to their songs and stories, and be amazed by the rich tapestries of other people, as he seeks to embrace them in his own admirable images and soaring music. With this volume, Farouk Sesay has advanced wonderfully as a poet and can lay claim to being one of the two or three finest Sierra Leonean poets of his generation.

Syl Cheney-Coker
Freetown, Sierra Leone
Author of *The Road to Jamaica* (SLWS 2015)

About this book

Nothing rattles me more than having to write about my writing so I have it as a rule not to write about my poems after they have been written; I believe a poem has a tone, tenor, mood and a life difficult to replicate in a prologue to a poem. Hence those that came out with a stuttering defect from my imagination or my stream of consciousness   to the paper stutters throughout their poetic life, those that came out with a limp are condemned to lurch throughout without crutches till they succumb to Gabriel Garcia Marcus's doomsday prediction; "the end of all—literature is the dustbin"

I am deviating from the rule this time to write something about this collection; the poems that made it here were written during a period of eight years that began immediately after the publication of my first collection of poems in 2007. The phrase made it appropriates the massacre of metaphor and slaughter of images that characterized the creative process which saw some poems abandoned and others decapitated.

My intention was to publish the whole lot in this collection but a senior poet; I gave the manuscript for editing advised against that with a logic predicated on several decades of experience in the field of writing and publishing poetry. So what you are reading is a down sized edition of what could have been the edge of a cry. The remaining poems will come in two separate volumes at a later date. I have also selected poems from my previous book; *Salute to the Remains of a Peasant,* to give the reader a sense of my journey into the realm of poetry.

What is novel about this publication is the fact that it includes two poems written in my local language Themneh. It is the freeing of the mind experienced in the process of writing in my mother tongue, which fulfills and liberates me. I had problems capturing the sounds of a tonal language in a standard autograph but the editorial intervention a renowned linguist Prof. Sheikh Umarr Kamarah put me out of my dilemma.

Nevertheless writing in my mother tongue took me to a place in my mindscape I never knew existed and with a supersonic speed I have never experienced. Now I know what pioneers like Ngugi Wathiongo meant when they talked about decolonizing the mind.

Some of the poems in this collection have never been published anywhere, others have been published in various media and others in anthologies like AFRIKA IM GEDICHT a German language anthology.

It is my hope that these poems would journey through minds and consciousness before they die like everything in this vast emptiness.

Prelude

Oumar Farouk Sesay writes from the margins while living in the middle of their daily invisibility.

These hidden margins seem to provide the walking path this poet use to take note of the places we pass unnoticed in the rush of our day, to remember the face of pain and joy even across continents, to hear the songbird when it sounds the minor note of dissonance and sadness, cousin of the forlorn flute.

The Edge of Cry enters alongside marginal spaces, listens for silence, and watches for the faceless. As wandering poet Farouk lets words arrive on paper from the inside out, unveiling his own hidden inner landscape, the liminal opening that feels the sound of the *Cry*.

I have followed Farouk's poetry across volumes and encounters. When he recites, his poems jump alive as if they needed reverberating sound to accompany the muteness of the page. In this extraordinary volume I cannot help but hear his voice lent to borderless flight of a poet at once deeply at home, at once traveling. Inevitably, the 'out there' brings him back -- whether

Colombia, Gaza or Michigan. His context remains and returns to Africa and Sierra Leone, land of birth and love, yet sweltered in 'the smell of her sweat' and reeking of 'toil on an arid soil' – for his heart lays close to ground, absorbing the 'beats between the heartbeats' of justice lost with a memory that refuses to forget and notices those in distant, foreign lands where the familiar is the way too many have faded to the margins.

In these pages we feel the yearning that wishes for a return back to normalcy or for a rapture that would shoot the poet away from 'frailty and to the galaxies, like an arrow.' This great human dilemma of wanting to go back to a more innocent lost time straddled with the desire to get beyond it all cannot misconstrue Farouk's pursuit of the *Edge* as escapism. The opposite bears out in the full reading. This poet has never shied from organic, at times excruciatingly descriptive images of rape, pillage, slave-like exclusion and the plight of daily survival of those who literally and figuratively break stones endlessly for a few crumbs of table bread.

No, *The Edge of the Cry* does not seek escapism. It does not follow the sounds till they disappear into nothingness.

These poems call for the courage to 'feel the fire of their undreamt dreams.'

Herein we find the genius of this volume. We come alongside the journey of the intrepid poet seeking the edge of the cry while still holding the saltiness of shared tears. Unafraid to say, 'just let me go.' Away from the strips of human bondage and harm -- if Gaza, if an old woman clinging to an empty calabash, if the nauseous sea spitting our own dirt back at us. Yet the poet keeps calling us back to real people, to daily dilemmas, to the human condition.

So let us go. Let us not be penned-up and confined by our weak and limited vision of human potential. But rather in our going let us take the courage of the poet: Notice the *edge*. Feel the *cry*. Take the pen. And bloom the flowers of friends and healing.

John Paul Lederach
Kroc Institute
University of Notre Dame

THE ANTHOLOGY WITHIN US

We all have poems buried deep within us
An anthology anchored on the banks of our souls
Sometimes buried so deep and fastened so firm
 it eludes the grasp of our minds
Sometimes the similes are severed,
Metaphors mangled and sonnet bayoneted
Ballads beaten to sound like a lament.
Wounded images strewn the soulscape
Like the massacre of Dresden

Amidst the wreckage in this vast mind field
The poems within us look like scraps
I work in the scrap yard of metaphors
I ravage every minefield in my mind
Like a possessed archaeologist
I excavate every artefact in my soul,
to bring you the poem buried in me
Then
 I see the heap of broken metaphors yearning for furnace
 to smelt the poem rusting inside you
Between your anxiety and anguish a line lies battered
Between your love and your hate, a paradox roams naked.
In the in- between of your joy and sorrow, a simile is strangled
In the shadow of your mind,
a silhouette of a homeless poem slumbers

There is a vast anthology in every one of us;
 anthologising the bits and pieces of our lives.
As I piece mine in strings of images and metaphors
 I see yours dripping blood from your wounded soul
I can smell the odour of your decaying metaphor
As it lies buried in a shallow haiku:

Still birth, in the cradle of conception
Yours! I can touch the texture from here;
It's dry and brittle, like a poem abandoned to the elements:
Yours blooms with colour and oozes with perfume
Blown by wind of hope and chaperoned by hyperbole
I feel all of your poems from here
And I yearn for my poems to dive in the coral reef of your soul
To mate with your poems into
 a single poem that speaks
 as an anthology of our poems !

SHE DANCED THAT DAY

She danced that day
On the sod of sadness-
Then a heap of sediments in my soul
She gyrated, undulated and spun,
raising dust marking my dust
My caged spirit grew wings and flew with her
to the nest of her song;
the source of her dance;
we waltzed and tangoed till we became one
My song a chorus to her song
My dance choreographed by hers
As I danced with her that day,
the thudding of her feet within me
left a song and a dance here
She danced that day
And I danced every day to celebrate her dance

THE EDGE OF THE OCEAN

Here I am, alone on the edge of the ocean
On the tip of dawn with a nomadic mind;
roaming distant landscapes, grazing fields and
scolding the waves for residual memory of verse
the wreckage of human experience left in it

Here I am alone hustling the wind
For a sigh of a muse blown away by the wind of antiquity
 or the anguish of a poet anchored in tranquillity
Or the curiosity of a lover crushed by the weight of waiting
or the anxiety of a mother tending the loss of a child
or the joy of a maiden maddened by the first touch of love
 To forge a line of a poem to feed my verse

Here I am feeling the pulse of the wind
Gauging the heart beat of the waves
For the vital signs of a stray line or even a lame metaphor
Or a rhyme ripped apart by rhythms of rage
or crippled simile crawling to reach the wheel chair of a poem
the poem I am forging just to mimic the vast epic
 sprawling in front of me.

The waves and the wind grind the loins of verses
 for lines to scream about the anguish of men,
who gave their last breath here.
The torment of those for whom this vast expanse of water
 is a grave, grabs the lapels of my soul.
I pulled, they pulled back,
 with all the might of their pain
 I pulled their pain with all the might of poetry,
strand by strand to weave their lives to mine
The futility of life, theirs and mine, mummified me.

I pulled my mind from the edge
and walked away from the sea's edge
Humbled

THE DEPARTURE

I stood in the lounge holding two hugs
lodged in the depth of my heart;
One for her humanity,
the other for what I should have said to her
That I didn't say
My mind condemned to a counterfactual Prison;
What could have happened?
Had I said what I should have said?
Cheery eyes as my hugs made faces at me and hug each other
Celebrating my dilemma
I stood lost in wonder of a world I had glimpsed at through
the window of her eyes
I frolicked in her forlorn look that tells tales of forlornness
spanning beyond remembered memory
Her smiles had scored songs into souls
and my soul dance foxtrot like it never danced before
Between her words and thought I took refugee
Wondering what could have happened,
had I said what I should have said
I cursed myself for not saying in words
What I had said several times since I saw her
And I dare to call myself a poet
But words wounded in the gauntlet of human emotions
And siege by norms have lost the capacity to appropriate
Feelings buried deep in layers and layers of human narrative

I stood in the lounge holding two hugs,
Fettered by rules, shackled by expectations as I contemplated
What could have happened? Had I said what I had wanted to
say.

A FORLORN FLUTE

Notes from a forlorn soul reached me today through a flute
as I was crouching on the edge of my nerves,
Each note carried the forlornness of souls of ages gone
The range stretched beyond remembered memory.
Minor notes on the heels of suspended notes
Drip epic of epochs gone.
The forlorn songs of shepherd's flutes, flung in distant places,
echo the unheard ballads lingering in the pastures.
The abyss of loss wails, like sirens of an odyssey,
dreams undone, drip like sound flakes
And hope, balanced on the tip of despair, clinked on every
note.
Notes from a forlorn flute reached the shores of my soul
Opening vistas of human triumphs and tragedies
Scooping every pulse of my being to feed the forlorn flute
Notes from a flute reach me from a distance
Turning me to a flute blowing a thousand flutes in my soul

MY POEM IN COLOMBIA

My poem went to Colombia via yahoo
On an all expense paid trip to give poetry might
It came back speaking with a soulful twang
in a language that lingers like a song
basking on a history; tap roots deep,
as memory on the cross road beeps.

My poem, enriched by a new language flourishes
with a single syllable of Spanish. I perish!
Colombia emboldens my poem with a bragging right.

I went to Colombia, following my poems footprint
via American air line, with a lot of carbon prints.
But my poem now speaks Spanish with elegance
While I stutter mangled syllables in ignorance
It walks on ' La casa de la memoria' with a swag
Dance salsa with sassiness that shocks,
When I could only manage to say buenas tardes
And I dance salsa- like yoga
muttering viva Colombia like a joker.

Compensating a Lang with a slang
I shout viva Colombia with a slant!

*House of memoria in Medellin Colombia

HUMANITY

Though they crossed paths every day in their quest to quench
Though they honked horns at each other every day in their
haste
Though they collided with each other every day in their
conflicts
Though they annoyed each other every day in their inpatient
Though they fought each other every day in their desire to
dominate
In separate but different ways they are inextricably bound to
each other like organisms
They either triumph together or are damned for all of eternity!

THE SONG OF THE WOMEN OF MY LAND

Like a sculptor chipping away at bits of wood,
Time chisels away bits of their memory

It strips away lyrics of the song of the women of my land
Leaving only a fading tune echoing the song,

they sang in the forlorn fields
  about their lives; songs
  of how they ploughed the terrain of their mindscape
  for memories of lyrics lost in the vast void of time,
in those days when a song beheld their lives;
when servitude cuffed the ankles of their soul,
and dereliction decapitated the epic of their lives.

With a song, they sponged off their anguish,
to behold their collective pain,
to celebrate their gains,
 give lyrics to the tune of their lives,
 cheat the tyranny of time,
 and commune with the yet unborn
to give meaning to an epoch lost in antiquity,

Yet time strips the lyrics and scars the tune,
leaving a dying song
Dead!
Like the women who died long ago,
Leaving the song to tell the story of their lives

Today the tune roams the forlorn fields
 Like their souls looking for lyrics

To tell the tale of the servitude
of the women of my land
Who ploughed their soil and soul
For a song to sing the story of their lives
The song of the women of my land
left in the memory of the wind.

Now feeding the verses of poets, it echoes in fields
Wriggling in rhythms and melodies,
Hollering in distant tunes
In places far afield from the forlorn fields,
where the song of their lives died.

The stuttering lips of my pen
And the screeching voice of my nib
try to sing the song of the women of my land
In verses far from the theatre of toil
 where they left a song that now roams the land
stripped of lyrics like a scorned ghost.
The tune tuning the tenor of my verse,
 is all that remains of the song of the women of my land
Who laboured and died leaving a dying song:

The dirge of their lives!

ON WRITING POETRY

I spent an entire Sunday trenching
the depth of my soul for nuggets of poetry
human history might have left in me
  I exhumed fossilized images entrenched in myths
  and dug for the poetry of my ancestry in my genome
The rhythm of my pulse I scored on my mind for rhymes
Then I scooped the landscape and skyscape;
trawled the ocean and soulscape for metaphors
  to quench my burning verse

Like I just built the pyramid alone,
  my strength sapped and my mind boggled.
I abandoned the computer and stumbled to my bed.
  My poem bleeds like an open wound
  in the gauntlet of the land,
  which has given a dagger to my poems;
Scars and scabs rage in my verse, a mad house thrives there!

  With a peasant's machete the lines
of my blistered hands flourish, and, the battle raging,
a warrior tossed a spear to my poems!

  Very much like my country's hurt,
  a torture chamber is in my soul
Despair grips me like my country, and
a wound, very much like my country's wound, bleeds
on this serene Sunday morning!
  My poetry frightened me
It tied me to the saddle of two mad horses
  bolting in different direction
If reading this tears you apart and burns you,
then spare a thought for me

for I was a furnace that Sunday morning
Burning to forge my country's hurt into a poem
Just to cool my frayed nerves.

ON READING Cheney Coker*

I sat on the edge of the ocean
Listening to the symphony of waves
Harping the chords of the shore
And responding to the shores of my soul
The water kissing the toes of my feet
  at the dawn of dawn
On the precipice of pain
  away from the storm of mankind.
Then your verse unveiled the veils
Veiling the secrets of life;
The ruse of wars
The specks we are in a vast canvass
The joy embedded in pain
The pain buried in joy
The death in the womb of birth
The birth in the tomb of death
The peace in war
The war in peace
The paradox at the core of our essence
All vaulted in your verse
And I marvelled at the depth of your mind
And the ocean

Syl Cheney- Coker: a leading Sierra Leonean poet and novelist

CHURH BELL AT REGENT*

On Easter Sunday, the bells of Regent toll,
a spirit of hope fills the village to the brim
over flowing to cottages in Charlotte and beyond
Serenity drapes the village, like a veneer of dew
Like those before them, the *Regentonians** clutched their bibles
And surfed the memory- laden wind over trodden paths
burdened with a palimpsest of foot prints of yesterday
and air perfumed with undone dreams
towards a church older than their memories.

A beacon maps a spiritual path
to resurrect the spirit of Regent nailed on the cross of change.
As they pray on that Easter Sunday, they pry on the memory
of the wind
to convey their prayers to those the Regent bells will toll for
tomorrow
Their spirit renewed, hopes lifted and prayers anchored on a
cross
 on the summit of Golgotha, across time and space,
Their Regent on the cross roads, their lives on the cross
They then return home, crossed by change,
 anchoring their hopes on the regency of man;
 on the cross of a distant past.

*Refers to residents of Regent village: one of the earliest settlements on the
hills overlooking Freetown*

I SAW THEM

I saw them today; droopy pants, foul tongues, blood shot eyes,
Those who would tread on the land after we are buried in it
I saw them today; depraved manners, disrespect for order,
Those who would pluck the fruit of the land after we became
manure
I saw them today; the elk of our posterity for whom we lost
our lives, posturing in the nude
I saw them today; the beneficiaries of our toil making mockery
of our heritage
I saw them today like they saw us yesterday; hip star pants, afro
hair, riff smoking
I saw them today as they will see them tomorrow;
Nude!
And I ponder over the purpose of our posterity pursuit in this
vast nothingness that begets nothingness till it steels to eternal
nothing

BETWEEN WINKS

My eyes spanned the sea of faces
surging in the lawn of *Bintumani*.*
Facescapes to mindscape, they marched
looking for familiar scapes in the landscape of my memories.
Suddenly her eyes met mine and mine met hers.
We stared at each other's soul; before we shook eyes
She winked at me and I winked back,
   to a past that lingers in our present;
   while casting a shadow to our future.

Between our winks,
   a flood gate of memories opened.
   Montage of memories flowed to every corner
Of our human shore
Between our winks, the epic of our past life
   was told in slides and shapes, in multiple shades.
We smiled at every slide and our eyes hugged;
we savoured the warmth of the hug
   before our eyes returned to our separate lives.
Yet our minds mused on what could have been
if we had shared the life we had yesterday.
Now buried in shades of time
On the canvass of our souls
And smiles, submerged in the volcano of our souls,
   erupted on our facescapes,
   bringing joy to every inch of our human estate

*A five star hotel in Freetown named after a mountain of the same name

DIARY OF THE LAST DAYS AT THE SEASONS RETREAT*

13th Sept 2013- 8pm
We are still here: I, Clifford, Carole and John Paul.
Covered by the warmth of your hugs
Smitten by your parting kisses
Listening to the silence of your meditations
And caught in the cross roads of your contemplations

We are still here, seated around the dining table,
Savouring words spiced with compassion we shared at dinner
time
Listening to your voices echoing in the chambers of our soul
Your laughter cracking walls of limitations
Your demeanour shredding barriers

We are still here, listening to the echoes of Tommy Sands
  singing wisdom- laden lyrics.
And Vanessa's soul piercing voice
And Ruben strumming his guitar
And Julie Okot Bitek's reflective poetry
And John's rendition of his Haiku
And Angie's soul shattering reading,
And Petr's piano notes ricocheting in our soulscape
And Alberto's classic rendition
 And Scott's humane narrative
And Krista's probing voice
 reaching the inner shores of our beings
And Barbara's deep insight
And Wendy's support
And Kirsten Rain's soul piercing verses
And Tom's silence conducting the orchestra of silence

in the trenches of our soul!

In the midst of the deafening silence
We reflect on the days we spent together, laugh like we laughed
that night
Before you followed your carbon footprints
  to your homes, leaving us here holding your memories.
We went to bed that night with heavy hearts and open minds!

14th Sept 8am
We are still here: Farouk, Carole and Clifford.
John Paul left that morning perhaps to stop the rain in
Colorado;
  leaving us with notes , hugs and compassion
We are still here, the last of the Ambassadors of compassion;
Who came across the globe to glue the pieces
of a broken world with compassionate presences

  We are still here, eating a breakfast of Yogurt
as cold as our hearts
  While the fists of our minds clench your thoughts.
  Our hearts hug your humanity,
And we hear the cringing of our souls
  as your thoughts question the essence of our existence

14th September 11 am
Carole and I left for Inns and Airports,
Leaving Cliff holding our hugs and thoughts
  We ponder over the bonds we made in just four days
and yearn to replicate that beyond the season.
We left the season filled with the absence of your presence
As we contemplate the presence of your absence within our
soul
A hotel at the Kroc Centre, in Kalamazoo, Michigan.

THE SEED
(for the Fetzer Centre)

In a part of town that runs away
 from the centre of town
On the edge of the running town
In a forest helmed by a lake
A seed fell from John Fetzer's mind;
It sprouts to a flora of stones and wood
Wooing minds to boom and blossom;
In seasons of fall, spring summer and winter
The bloom brims with pollen
Wafting away from mind to mind
 cross pollinating a garden of ideas
in the mindscapes of humanity;
a flora of compassion was born;
 some sing the tale of their compassion in a song ,
 others sculpture their compassion in poems
Some narrate in stories and anecdote
Others tell in petals of hope
Some tell in science of waves
Yet others tell in silence;
To reclaim compassion
To foster forgiveness
To better humanity
Just like the seed that fell from John Fetzer's mind

TODDLERS

We were toddlers then
Toddling with joy in our school yard;
Kicking, screaming, skiing, jumping in our paradise
Yearning to yarn a world like our school yard world
We were so innocent and pure even in our fights
We played and prayed for a brighter future
Then the future came years later;

And in that future, our playmate
Idris jump to his death
from a tower building in Canada,
wanting the kind of love
we had in the playground.

And in that future, Kanu perished in prison
Longing for the compassion in our playground

We didn't know that in that future, Shekito
would be executed at Pademba prison
for murder, wishing he had lived
like we lived in our little paradise

Yet, in that same future,
Solomon became a scientist researching
for a cure to rid the world of malaria
And Tudi became a nurse
Tending body and soul with love and compassion
Just like we had in the playground

And Gibril became a poet,
Sieving his country's pain
In filters of metaphor

We did not know that the world
And our toddler world were   worlds apart
Because we were just toddlers
Toddling in our little paradise

VISTA-NURSING HOME

When they were younger they carried the dream with pride
They fed and nurtured the dream with memories of the
Gettysburg address
the pain of Pearl Harbour, the inspiration of Abraham Lincoln,
The vision of George Washington and the hopes of the land of
the free and home of the brave

As they grew older,
They fought their own Pearl Harbour
They made their own Gettysburg address
and carried America on their shoulders;
America carried them in her womb.
But the might was so great it snapped their nape,
bent their bodies,
And sometimes maimed their spirit
Dumped in this place with severe love,
they limp with crouches and roll in wheel chairs,
thinking of the weakness the greatness has left them with:
a dream that breaks and eludes

Their bodies tired and soul subdued
Their spirit maimed and their hope harked
The radiance of the dream had dimmed their eyes
Their loved ones gone to chase their dreams
And they are left to battle solitude
In the hands of care givers they never dreamt of
In the days when the dream was a dream

THE OASIS OF ABERDEEN

She sat on the sidewalk she called a patio
of an X-marked shanty home;
a cigarette dangling from her lips.
Nude, like her life, She waits for eviction,
either from her makeshift shelter
or from life, whichever came first.
She had ceased to care long ago,
when her life started to burn like cigarette.
The smoke lingers and fades away,
Just like the ashes of her life.
   Now she perishes on the side- walk,
where she walked her cat walk
amidst a cacophony of cat calls!

This belle was once the oasis of Aberdeen:
 Men came from the toil of casting nets,
and rowing ships, to drink from her oasis.
Her body was an assembly of nations:
Korean; north and south, Chinese and Tibetans,
Israelis and Palestinians: all came to quench their thirst.
They drank from her oasis for dimes
 until the dame was dammed,
to live wretched on a side- walk
where she was once a queen.

   Today the luring lustre is gone,
 like the azure green of Aberdeen's shore;
the glossy skin bleached to lure men
is now scaled like a lizard's skin.
   And the glean in the hazel eyes dimmed and sunk in sockets.
The once beautiful face is now a grand canyon without
spectacle;

and cavities punctuating the cigarette stained teeth,
complete the ruin of the queen of Aberdeen!

She has nothing to show for the days of her reign:
 Not a home; not even a bastard son
Who would return one day, gun in hand,
 embittered by scorn, teased for his ancestry,
to shoot her for making him a plutonic bastard!

A LITTLE BOY

He sat by the road side
By an unfinished hut
Starring at a rice nursery
His stomach ploughed by hunger
His hunger stared back at him
As he contemplated how he could be fed
By a nursery of rice in an unfinished hut
In the middle of nowhere
His hunger remembered yesterday's hunger
And imagined tomorrow's hunger
And the pangs in his stomach
Recalled the pangs that brought him
To this void of vastness
Tears dripped from his eyes as he mourned
The plight of those coming after him to
Inherit this plight of blight
in the midst of plenty

JUST LAST NIGHT

Just last night T boy bled to death
under the Kaningo Bridge,
fired at for stealing a bunch of bananas.
Just last night J man was electrocuted at Ross road
trying to steal cables from grid lines.
Just last night teenagers thronged a film house watching ex-
rated movie
Just last night three children raped a teenage girl;
 re-enacting a scene they saw in a porn movie.
Just last night four youths were killed in an armed robbery at
Spur road
Just last night another was killed by a falling container as he
rode on his *okada**

Just last night another youth died in dire straits at the
Connaught hospital
Just last night Raka was killed in election violence
Just last night Alagaba slept on the street
 with his dreams drowning in sewers of despair
Just last night others were marking their hopes and aspiration
on mercury lottery papers
Just last night Alimamy, starved of justice,
died in pademba prison for loitering
Just last night we were riddled with guilt for neglecting the
future generation
And just this morning we dared call them future leaders of
tomorrow
when we let them die like flies.

Okada- commercial bike

THE MAN IN MY POEM

He was a mere man when first I saw him;
  meandering on the margins of my metaphor
tiptoeing on the ridges of my images
Marginalized
Later, I saw the solitary man in my poem
He had grown from being a metaphor
Of my country's pain to a poem of pain
Replete with metaphor, oxymoron, similes and irony
He wore his anguish and that of his kind
As he agonized how he had grown from a line
To stanza from stanza to a poem speaking the torment of the
land
His lost limb an anthology of his country's war years
His nagging hunger a tragic epic of the peace time war
His severed spirit like a caged bird singing a melancholy song
His memory a waste land of broken dreams oozing puss
His broken hopes limped on crouches of reed
The man-poem walks past me smelling like the great
unwashed,
publishing his poems on the conscience of the land.

ODE TO SADNESS

(Inspired by a poem of the same title written by Pablo Neruda)

Hydra- headed serpent sailing the wind of pain
Across seas of torment to shores of grief
Seeping moments of joy from souls arid by strain
leaving a trail of sadness.
Don't you dare trespass my moment of joy
 With tear drops
And metaphors of souls clutching bullets
And cries of anguish drowned in eulogies.

Today a muse of joy lives here
With wedding bells ringing
And tales of love looming
Sadness don't you dare toll these bells
With pain and grief by crossing these frontiers

Your bitterness will be filtered till the sweetness
Embittered in your rampage pours
 Like milk from suckling cow,
  to feed nomads
Saddened by the hurricane you unleashed.
Sadness, don't you dare cross this path
 Because, poised to celebrate joy, a poet lives here
Sadness don't cross this path.
 Like Pablo Neruda on the shores of Chile,
 I shall rob you of your integrity,
  And forge an eternal ballad from your remains,
for lovers saddened by your frolic.

Your armour of steel will be burnt in a furnace
 Hammered to a pot to cook meals

For orphans starved by the war you waged

Sadness don't you dare cross this frontier
It's a joyous fortress fortified by a poet
Emboldened by your tyranny to write a poem of joy

RAPE

I.

We turned the bodies of our women into battlefields
Firing at them with *chakabulars** propped between our legs
Scaring their wombscape like *Ruffian** killing fields
The sweats from the brow of their soul drowned their bodies
We were an invading army looting the obelisk of their Ethiopia
The embers of our loins scorched the sacredness of their being
And the fires of our lust consumed the oasis of their soul

Cheered by depravity anchored on the pendulum of our loins
We beat our chests on their breasts to test our manhood.
The vows to die for their honour faded in the cacophony of
our moans
 Echoes of the ecstasy of shame prowled in the cages of our
emptiness
 On the summit of their memories we hoisted the flag of
shame.
 Fluttering and fanning the fires of hate, we stoke in their souls
For the army suckling succor from their breasts
While defiling the milk with the bile of our chakabulars

II.

From Darfur to Congo to Rwanda to Kailahun
 Soldiers of shame limped across the continent soaked in
shame
Sapping the allure of the muses of negritude
Hiroshima of contempt we placed underneath the core of their
soul
Exploding everyday to multiple Hiroshimas in their mindscape
Shame bowed down in shame
for the wars we fought on the bodies of women
The trenches we dug in their soul
The *estu brute* wounds we left in their wombs

With weapons of old forged in the furnace of their wombs
We raped them with chakabulars
And raped them again with the penises of our tongues
The stigma left blisters of shame on their image
Like the blisters we left in their wombscape
And their bodies, now a battle field with wreckages of arsenal,
Burning!!! Burning!! Burning!

III.

But from the ashes, the phoenix of African womanhood rises
From the verses of Isis the resurrection beckons
From the pyramid of Egypt Cleopatra came on the heels of
Nefertiti
From the sacred groves of *Sandathanka* the ankle bells of
Nasomayla struck
From the Peninsular Casely- Hayford's pen rages
From the rice fields and fishing ports they came chanting
From the shackles of forced marriages they break free
From Angola Queen Nzinga rallied the amazons
From Ashanti Ya Asantewaa raised the flag of pride
From Zaria Queen Amina shouts the command
To reclaim the milk of life we defiled
To gather the souls we scattered
To piece together the calabash we smashed
To redraw the sacred lines we crossed
To reclaim the territory we invaded
To return the obelisk we looted
To replace the beacons we uprooted
To reassert the honor we dishonored
To Nile the oasis we drained
And to wage a war in the landscape of our soul
They came wearing the scars of the battle of our birth like
medals
The breast milk we defiled drenched the battlefield
The battle cries of estu Brute fill the air

The cries numbed our soul
The chakabulars went limp
We retreated like eunuchs spoiled with the spoils of our war of
shame
And the loot of our burnt image
Saddled on the wounded camels of our souls

*Reference to the rebel of the Revolutionary United Front (RUF) who
waged an eleven years brutal war in Sierra Leone*

A local gun fabricated by locally artisans

A LETTER TO GLADYS CASELY-HAYFORD

"Freetown, when God made thee, He made thy soil alone
Then threw the rich remainder in the sea.
Small inlets cradled He, in jet black stone.
Small bays of transient blue He lulled to sleep
Within jet rocks filled from the Atlantic deep.
Then God let loose wee harbingers of song.
He scattered palms profusely o'vr the ground
Then grew tall grasses, who in happy mirth
Reached out to kiss each palm tree that they found.
"This is my gem!"God whispered "this shall be
To me a jewel in blue turquoise set"
Thus spake the mouth of life's eternity;
There tranquillity lies Freetown, even yet.
The God couched, lion-like, each mighty hill.
Silent, they keep their watch over Freetown still
Silent- "
Gladys Casely- Hayford

Dear Gladys Casely-Hayford
Sorry to wake you up from your eternal sleep
But I need to tell you about the Freetown
You immortalized in your poem;
The Freetown you said God made with rich soil
and the remainder he threw to the sea:
the one God said was a jewel in blue turquoise set:
the Freetown of small bays of transient blue
And jet rocks sprouting
With dancing grass kissing the forest
And lion like mountain crouched keeping watch
Well, Casely, since you left for eternity,

the God- made Freetown is gone to eternity
and your poem now reads like a eulogy
and your imagery of beauty echoes like the chant of a
delusional poet
whose state of mind harkens back to Pedro Da Cintra,
a drunken sailor who thought mountains were lions
and miss- named a country; Sierra Loya

Casely, man's quest to quench his wants
has given your Freetown a drastic make over.
Your sprouting jet rocks; hauled and crushed
to build edifices of ugliness on the manes of your lions.
The transient blue is now everything;
and the dancing grass that kissed the forest
dances no more.
Chopped off and burnt for fuel
to cook the cholesterol that blocks arteries,
there is no forest left to kiss now.
Its thirsty voice exacts revenge
for what they did to the landscape.
At Aberdeen Greek, they have choked the lungs of the ocean
with shacks of zinc and rust spread under the sun,
leaving the ocean gasping for breath.

The breeding Greek breeds death,
the crouching lion mountain is mortally wounded,
and left to bleed during the August torrent,
eroding the rich soil to feed the sea.

Your poem now reads like a license to lie
commissioned by poetic license
The poets of the land rose to defend your poem
But the poetry of trees, the music of nature
The harbingers of song

That gave a soul to your poem are gone
The poets scavenged bald mountains for trees and dancing grass,
They trawled a blue- less sea for the transient blue
They scooped a sound scape for a song
 and returned from a harvest of metaphors with bare souls,
to mourn the Freetown you captured in the lenses of your metaphor

The harbingers of song flutter
like vultures hovering over the carcass of your Freetown.
 and your silence is shattered by a thousand honking horns
 even on Easter Sundays.
"This is my slum" a man whispered; "this shall be to me
A slum in slime set."
Slums ate the forest and water ways
and poisoned the soul of the avenging poems
The aperture of their metaphor opens but only to capture
a different canvass of time
a changed landscape
 a different people.
The truth is, Casely, we killed your Freetown.
The wood from the forest we made to funeral pyre
We dance the dance of death around the fire
The rocks we gorged to wipe her memory
Then from the ashes, we built ours,
and made your poem an epitaph
we placed on the tomb stone of the God- made Freetown;
we sang a requiem for you and your Freetown;
 God be with you till we meet again; rest in peace

POETRY STONE

The stone I wrote a poem on
was gorged from the core of the earth,
 and rolled down the hill to the roadside,
away from the deep boulders holding the hills of Leicester
from spewing rage on men,
 disembowelling the earth;
leaving bleeding sores on the core

Crevices clutching tales of time
Lacerate the rock like wrinkles
Laying bare stories buried in the earth's crust

The stone bears wounds left by stone breakers
 who butchered the stones
like cadaver poet looking for metaphors

It tells the tale of the withering hill
eroding away to the gullies below
And the lumbering of trees
Exposing the hill to the lashing of time

Time chirps away bits of the stone
Changing history at every stroke
Until a stroke brought men of voids
Striking rocks with fire for bread

The stone lie on the roadside waiting
for ears to hear her poetry of pain
 musing in the abyss of time,
when man and nature entwine.

No machine will lumber away the logs
or stones gorged and rolled
on the roadside epitaphs,

for a landscape in the throes of death
The mute poet will stutter verses of doom,
to the morticians of gloom:
  Poems of doom
  the stone hurled to me-a panting poet
passing a bald forest
scared !

"Remember the Charlotte landslide
Behind the hills of Leicester"
  whispering to me, a tired poet chasing a muse,
and listening to the mute stone muttering
a subterranean poem for the deaf,
as I contemplate a poem on the poetry stone

MASINGBI

1

This place, this town,
Scattered on hills, dumped in valleys
 Laced with streams helmed by swamps
Tilled by toiling peasants, serenaded by birds
and left on the cross roads of culture.
Like fankandama* to the gods.

This place ,gave birth to me on a Sunday dawn.
The Muezzin lashed the silence of dawn with azan
The tolling Church bell rang across the land
And Grandma's sambore* scuttled between the bell and the azan
In that saturated sonicscape, my induced cry squeezed in between,
A chorus of cheers and laughter drowned the cry
Startling the birds nestling on a tree next to grandma's house
Then benediction to Allah
Then Incantation and libation to ancestors celebrated my birth

2

Neneh Oumou, tired of a maiden birth,
dozed off in grandma's bed with a smile.
They pinched me again, I cried and they laughed
The ambience of joy and the allure of communion of candies
 lured my elderly siblings, Ibrahim and Imran
From sleep, and they sprinted towards the church
Leaving the presence of their absence in the fajr saffa*
A cane left a memento on their backs, like hieroglyphs

Marking the day they scorned the Azan for the bell
And my natal day they carried on their backs in lieu of a birth
certificate.

I was a newborn new like an unwritten scroll
But memories as old as human history were written on my
tabula rasa
Punctuated by instinct of antiquity wired to my brain;
Patented with their memories,
 they staked their propriety claims on me
Each of them scored their song in my soul;
They wrote their poetry in my veins
Their gait and grace fed my essence
Their thoughts and beliefs fed my mind
There song and dance choreographed my rhythm

3

Two hundred infant strides
separated my father's house and grandma's
My toddler feet stitched the distance several times a day
making a single home out of two
Yet a gulf of beliefs separated both homes;
In grandma's house libation was followed by incantation
Salutations; *Nasolese okera, Nasofenthe okara**
In my father's house salats followed takbirs
Salutations : *assalamualiku mualakumsala**

4

My mind embraced the enormity of the contrast;
scooping compassion and harvesting love
to create an in- between world.
Between the in- between world,

amidst a multiple heritage, and a contested sonicscape,
I built my world with the whole
and the broken of both worlds
I salvaged the disused images
and gave sanctuary to the drifters and dregs
Then one day a riot began deep in the trenches of my being ;
Abuses hauled, fence broken, obscenities spewed
Then poetry came and restored order to my embattled estate

This is the story of the birth of my poetry

5

Soon, the chants began to coalesce into a single song
All the salutes became a single salute
Grandma's salute of okera orkara
Made its way into my verse
when I salute the remains of peasants
I salute her memory
The lullabies fed my verse with lyrics
Leaving scars of alterations and assonance
The sounds of that Sunday dawn buried deep in my sonicscape;
The azan and the bell erected a mosque and a cathedral
Within me yet tolerating grandma's shrine
The tweeting birds gave a bird to my poetry
that flies the shores of my soul
And sometimes singing a solitary song
to men sowing solitude in their souls
and sometimes limping across the sky of familiar hurt
with a broken wing,
 singing the song of Angelou's caged bird
The peasants brought hoes and machetes to my verse
they ploughed my poetry, they pruned my field of metaphor

the string of streams irrigated my poems and flow to the river
Rokel
and emptied to the Atlantic ocean bringing the lament of the
Middle Passage to my verse
Now my poem is melancholy a cry of pain fill her lungs

6
The women of my land :Nasolehse, Nasofenthe, Nasomayla
left a song in my poems that roam.
 Now only a fading tune remains to tell the story of their lives
the peasants of my land left sweat rivulets,
 blistered hands and scared feet in my poems
I took their poems beyond the borders of their existence
Across shores to water the field of human compassion

I came back to this place for more but the streams are gone
The swamps dried up
The women of my poems buried with their song
And the living: Open tombs on their faces
My poems starved of the Masingbi that fed it yesterday
I held my poems in the arms of my mind
And mused on the immortality of time;
 time had chewed the town
And spat it out on my face like kola nut spittle.
 I pick the pieces to remake a town that made me a poet

fankandama*- assorted sacrifice made to appease the gods or
God
sambore* a drum played during traditional initiation
ceremonies and feast
fajr saffa*- a straight line of worshippers
okera/okara- ritual form of greetings by women of esoteric societies*
: *assalamualiku mualakumsala** - *Arabic greetins adapted by most
muslims in Sierra Leone*

AFTER

After they would have disembowelled the land
And rip her entrails like a hyena will do to a prey
After they would have exhumed the ore and gold in her womb
And leave a trail of tombs
After they would have extracted the bauxite
And leave behind a gaping wound in our coffee farm
After they would have moved our village from its ancestral anchor
 to a desecrated part of the forest
After y they would have exhumed our ancestors leaving us to
endure the wrath of their scorned spirit
After they would have mutilated the genitals of culture leaving
us to bleed like an open sore
After they would have erased all our taboos and limitation
leaving us bare
Like bared foot dancers on embers of fire
After they would have raped our dignity and stole our integrity
Leaving us draped in self deprecation
After they would have turned the lush forest to wasteland
And leave a barren land to vomit our seeds
After they would have left us chained to poverty of the soul
and spirit
After they would have left to celebrate the gains
While we cringe in pain
After they would have polluted all our sources of water
And we are left to echo the cry of the ancient mariner;
"Water everywhere and nor any drop to drink"
After they would have left our Rokel river as a burning inferno
like the Cuyahoga River and we are left at its bank spitting

spittle to quench the fire
After they would have poisoned the air we breathe and we are
left gasping for breath in pockets of air
After we would have stop the bickering about our differences
And see the uniformity of our anguish
After all became like the wasteland of the final trumpet
We would realize that we have destroyed our paradise
This time with eyes wide open and mind firmly shot

URCHINS

Urchins pluck from their sleepless sleep
 lurched bear footed on rugged path,
balancing pales of water like donkeys.
Their thudding feet dance a dirge
For dreams decapitated on the edge of slumber
They clutch hunger in the fury of their stomachs
And needs nestled in their arteries
As they lynch consciences of workers
Saving children in air conditioned jeeps

FREETOWN

A sprawling city nestled between mountains and the ocean
Meandering through ridges snaking on contours and gorges
To lay her braided head on the Lion Mountain
And her pedicured feet in the bowl of the ocean
Yet morticians of mortar left the mountains bald
And the ocean choked with waste eroded from the mountains
Spewed slime on the beaches
The bald mountains then mocked the thirsty dam in revenge

LEICESTER PEAK

The wind rush into my lungs
As I lust in the lustrous green of Leicester Peak;
Serenaded by butterflies flapping their wings like accordion
Twittering birds titter in the everglades of my soul
Foliage swing in the wind
 like the fingers of a maestro on the keyboard
I hear the waning fog harping notes of solitude
My soul dances a love dance: The sambore dance:
The harvest dance.
The hands of my soul send the sickle sky high
 to the distant rhythm of the kelain
 Catching it I cut a swathe of happiness
 and smell the freshness
as I lust in the lustrous green of Leicester Peak
 on the eve of her baldness

I SAW YOU ON TV

On history channel,
I saw Martin Luther King
 clutching a bullet and a dream
as he descended to eternity
On biography channel,
I saw Mandela crushing
 the stone heart of Botha,
 like the stones of Robben Island.
On Geography Channel
I saw Wangari Mathia
dodging bullets to plant a tree .
On sky spot
I saw Jessie Owens sprinting
 and spiting the Aryan theory with his feet
On Cable News Network
I saw Barrack Obama
reading the epitaph to human folly
in Auschwitz camp
On Open University channel
I saw Wole Soyinka,
 and Derek Walcott
sharing metaphors

I mused at the pace of a race
That rose from the ashes of slavery
and the shackles of humiliation
I was filled with pride
Then I saw you without notice
 plastering your face,

My face
Our faces
Their faces
 and the face of negritude
with a gratifying grin
on America most wanted;
 As if you won the Nobel Prize!

That face is our brand
The face of our struggle
The face we hoisted on the arc of history
The face of our triumph
Not yours alone to be desecrated
On America's most wanted

THE BEACH

The sea spews rot on our shores
 Plastic sheet,
Syringes and surgical waste shit on the shores eyes
Condoms tangled with mesh of synthetic hair
 Horns studded with Shebes* in bottles
 scattered like mines
Our mangled shrapnel mess spills like slime
Choking the throat of the sea;
 The nauseous sea throws up on us.
We spew back
And she back

The sea fumes and farts.

On the shores of the sea
Our shit comes back without plastic sheet

Shebes*- charms sheathed in leather

KANINGO RIVER

Cheney, today I saw the remains of Kaningo:
the home of your muse
The Euphrates of your soul reduced to a river of sewage
like Samba Gutter* in the rains
Waste clogs his tributaries like sewage in sewers
Debris drowns the face of Kaningo in a river of dirt.
 Rot floods the river to the cheering of flies
And the disdain of butterflies
The Iguana of Kaningo swimming in your poem
 Is now a metaphor in an anthology of cassava leaves
 The schools of fish have degenerated to tadpoles wriggling in feces

Kaningo: a Euphrates no more
 but an open tomb for dog cadavers.
 Vultures devour your kingfishers,
 and keep vigil over the bile of vile streaming to the ocean.

11

Years ago, the birds flew to the sanctuary of your garden
Plotting a last stance against the forest of rot eating Eden

Like the gory locks of the madman at the High Commission
Kaningo's rage erupted in downpours, drowning the shanties
in the sewage,
to reclaim his home now dwelling only in your verse

He writhed in stench as they starved him with their anal sword

Conjuring his water to urine with filth wedged between their
legs
Filth which earlier conjured this semen of sins now sinning
Kaningo
The spirit of Kaningo lurched towards the open sea
And Kaningo River became a river without a spirit
Just like the body of humanity without a soul transforming him
into a sewer
The Euphrates of your poem is now a gutter less than Samba
Gutter*

Cheney, I saw the remains of Kaningo today waiting for your
eulogy

Samba Gutter-a massive drainage that streaks across the city of
Freetown and empties into the Ill-famous Kroo Bay

Kaningo is a male spirit after which the river was named

THE EDGE

This is the tale of a village on the edge of the Rokel river
And a villager who listens to the sounds of
Broken twigs, chirping birds,
Rising tides, kissing the lips of the river bank,
Wince of rescinding night
The horn of an antelope announces the dawn
Of rhythmic pounding of pestles in mortars
And songs of maidens pounding laundry,
To the beat of their forlorn hearts
They yearn for love ones in battle fields
And the choir of departing souls
with a melody, like that of the owl of the night

Ceremonies, cajoling the gods to bless the land,
Keep the villager listening; watching bronzed muscles,
And women burdened with bondage bending grave wards
Drums of rite of passage rumble,
hearts fumble
As they die under the knife of womanhood
to be buried with stigma in sacred bushes

The villager feels the same things:
The chilly harmattan wind drifting with the souls of ancestors
Storm carrying the rage of forefathers
And lashing the thatches of homes
He feels the pimples growing from embrace of ancestors
Roaming the spirit world

He touches skins dried by the sun;

scared by thorns and razor leaves
as they plough a hostile land
He feels the brutal hunger ravaging children in the august rain
And the torment of women trapped in unwanted marriages

They smell of sweating bodies
Mixed with decayed dreams hung over huts
Like morning dew on flowers
The fresh wind made moist by the river fills his lungs

All of these experiences linger in his mind
Waiting to be anchored in a poem
Or painted on canvass for posterity
But a mind maimed by ignorance stifles inspiration,
limping only to a syllable of a lame poem:
"Oh dunia,the world nor level"
With that masterpiece in his mind
He seats on the edge of the village
Remaking a world unmade by ignorance

POEM OF THINGS AND OTHER THINGS

A littered mind
A disused thought
A muffled song
A caged bird
A pregnant mind
A failed state
A confluence of pulse
A metaphor of martyrs
An angry poet
An unwritten poem
A poet unborn
A blind bat
A rotten mango
A tethered cow
A fossilized dream
A roaming ghost
A dead hero
A hacked limb
A chopped spirit
A stumped monument
A fading memory
An embalm body
A mummified soul
A tortured child
An abused woman
A dead rat
A wagging tale

A stunted metaphor
A broken pencil
A torn paper
A maimed muse
A stupid poet
A lame reader
A dead country

THE EDGE OF A CRY

On the edge of the road
 Fringes of the margins
Of a wretched existence lie
 Glued to her calabash, an old woman,
Leans on a dying pole,
Her muscles twitching
 Like a cringing guitar.

 Like a battered flute
Her arteries flutter
And bones clink
like clanking coins.
They are the sounds of her body
in that bowl
 A melancholy melody of pain;
Of a life steeped deep in penury!
Pain!

She wails for her mother
In a twisted note on the edge of her cry:

An octave lower than   muffled sound,
For the mother who gave birth to her,
Decades ago, in the midst of pain,
Echoing the same harrowing cry
Like her great grandmother cried

 On the margins of life
 Her pain caresses   every nerve
and fills her with nothingness.

Numbed by norms, she contemplated in her anguish,
the many years sculptured into her being ,
now reduced to nothing

By the chiming of time!

At the edge of the road,
With an empty calabash,
She lives on   an empty stomach:
 A life of void!

Like the women before her,
Who have re-echoed this same cry
In moments of pain
She wails for her mother:
 The pain of penury
Pinning her down
In a world   of dark void!

Again she cries,oh mimama tiday!

Kʌ pəmp ka ʌrɔŋ

Ka tʌyɛr ta ro gbantani
Ka ʌŋesəm ʌsɔmpanɛ
ɔya ubʌki ɔ manthlanɛ ʌŋpɛpɛ ŋɔŋ
ɔ sɛlɛ ka ʌŋənt ʌthey
mʌbay mɔŋ mə yʌr mɔ a fer ʌgbolu
ʌnəntha dɔŋ də pʌrpʌrnɛ mɔ a feŋ kəthɛma kə mɛpthanɛ
ɛbʌnth yɔŋ ɛyɔnɛ gbonklo gbonklo mɔ a fʌk ʌkala rʌ
ʌkonkofo
ʌder mɔ ʌbolpan ʌfoth
ʌŋesəm ʌnɔsinɛ mɔ ʌleŋ ŋʌ bayti
ŋesəm a gbəthəs ka ɔbaŋ wa ʌmɔnɛ
ɔ thʌl ɛrɔŋ ta yakɔŋ kom kɔ e
yɛ rim rə gbelgbel
ɔ gbʌsʌ ka kʌpəmp ka ɛrɔŋ

Rim rə boma də fənthʌ do ratha ka ɛrɔŋ
Ta ɔya kɔŋ kom kɔ e ʌyamani ʌbɔli
ɔya kɔŋ ɔ la sɔ thʌl ɛrɔŋ mɔ ɔkʌrʌbom kɔŋ ɔya kɔŋ
ɔ thʌl ɛrɔŋ ta ʌŋesəm a gbʌp ka tʌyɛr e
ɔ malanɛ ɔbaŋ ka ʌnəntha da ʌnesəm
ɛrɔŋ ɛ la thʌp yʌ ɔfoth wa ʌŋesəm
Yʌ mʌ gbɔŋknɔ ma tʌkur ta ʌŋesəm
ʌlana ʌbɔli ɔbaŋ wɔŋ a path ka ʌŋesəm ʌfoth e
Ka kʌpəmp ka ʌrɔŋ
Yɛ pɛpɛ ɛfoth-ʌŋ
Yɛ kor kəfoth-ʌŋ
Yɛ ŋesəm ʌfoth-ʌŋ
ɔya ubaki ɔ thʌl ɛrɔŋ ta ɔya kɔŋ

Mɔ wathubɛra təmʌ kɔ kədi e
ɔ la po thʌl ɛrɔŋ e
Ta ɔbʌki taŋ kɔ rʌ leŋ e
Ka ɔbʌki taŋ kɔ yʌ ɔfoth ka ɔfoth.
ɔ kʌl thʌl ɛrɔŋ:
"woyo ya kʌ mi thonɔŋ."

A BIRD

A bird whispers a song into my soul
Singing of bygone `days of men come and gone
And a choir of foliage and bird
now decommissioned
The soulful song brings memories
Of days when the birds had a choir
But a forest of concrete
Shrubs of steel
And foliage of zinc
evicts the choir of birds
Today a bird sings a solo song
In bald forest with a solitary tree
To men sowing solitude in their souls

ʌbʌmp

ʌbʌmp ɔ fofla ʌleŋ ka rʌwuni rʌ mi
ʌleŋ ŋʌ ʌyamani po thas-e
ŋʌ ʌkʌbilɛ po thase-e
ʌleŋ ŋʌ ɛgbɔfɔŋ yɛ
ɛ bʌmp a po kʌti ka kʌ leŋ e
ʌleŋ ʌ nɔsinɛ kʌrʌ mətʌmtʌmnɛ mʌ ʌlɔkɔ
ɛbʌmp aŋ ba met-e
kɛrɛ ʌgbɔnkɔ ŋʌ thonos
yʌ ʌgbɔfɔŋ ŋʌ ɛfʌt
ʌgbɔnkɔ ŋʌ ɛpan
A po sakthi ʌ met ma ɛbʌmp
Thonɔŋ ɛbʌmp anleŋ ʌleŋ ŋə rəson
Rʌ ʌgbɔŋkɔ ʌ kəthɛnth yɛ ŋənt ŋin-ʌŋ
Rʌ afəm akəpet mə sak ɔnɔsinɛ
Ka ɛŋesəm yaŋ-e.

I WANT TO GO

I want to go
Just let me go
Away from chains
To forest rain
Like a sparrow

Just let me go
Away from frailties
To the galaxies
Like an arrow

Just let me go
Away from greed
To creed
Like a believer

Just let me go
Away from hunger
To blooming flowers
Like a sunbird

Just let me go
Away from deception
To womb perfection
Like a child unborn

Just let me go
Away from prison
To ancestral reason
Like a spirit scorned

I want to go
Just let me go
Away from pens
To the pen
Like a poet
Just let me go

TO WOMEN I SAW RUSHING TO THE HOSPITAL

Maps of agony on faces with wrinkles like ridges
tears of anguish made tributaries
Like a Nile across the Sahara.
Bacons of pain on facescape: Spirit stuttering
Hope limping

They ran in the rain with Umbrellas under armpit
Head ties knotted round waists
Eyes blaring torment like a broken ambulance
As they ran to the direction of hospitals
Mummified to a morgue by a mob of morticians
 On oath to rip off lives

A CRY FOR MADDIE
(for Madeleine McCann)

I hold a cry in my soul
ebbing through the tears
Surging forth from tunnels of turmoil

Shoring in the inners shores of my being
Where the hollering of stolen children
Stole my soul like their stolen soul

I hold a cry for Maddie rumbling like a quake
To spew the torment of stolen children
Buried in a cemetery of inhumanity
Where the vicar of our silence keep vigil

I hold a cry for the pain ravaging her mother
As she lives in shadows
Embracing shadows,
Chasing silhouettes
And singing lullabies with the note of a dirge
For her living yet dying child
And dying yet living Maddie

I hold a cry for the unspoken word
Between her mum and Dad
As they talk without talking
And shout in their silence
And wake in their sleep
And sleep in their wake
And die in their living
And live in their dying

I hold a cry for Maddie as she woke up at night,
In the vast tomb of inhumanity
Shifting debris to glimpse at the twinkling star
And sending desolate cry to a mum
Clutching a festering hope
Like the sores in our conscience

I hold a cry for the moment of her waking up
In the tomb of inhumanity
To live the death of a stolen child
I hold a cry for the lie they told her
And a cry for the hurt the lie left in her

I hold a cry for the parents
As they reconstruct the world on wishes;
Piling guilt in their soul for living life
As Maddie pine in the hands of evil

I hold a cry for the "crumb de la crumb"
Making a living in the dying of stolen children
And a cry for the unanswered cry
Of Maddie crying out to us
As we tuck our Maddies in bed with kisses
While she contends with a serpent hiss
As her kiss waste in an empty room

THE SOUL OF MY COUNTRY

I look for it every day:
The soul of my country
in the unwritten epitaphs:
 Soul carved on broken tablet, and
 buried in the cemetery of time.

I look!
In the songs of desolate hearts:
those singing ballads that echoes like eulogies
across the wilderness of the soul,
In the mortars of immortality
the chorus of pestles pounding *furrah** for the dead
does not ring with the soul of my country

I look for it everyday
The soul of my country:
Rivulets of sweat,
gushing from the brows of proud men
and the groans of women dying in child birth,
mirrors the soul of my country.

In the last breath of the unborn,
I look for the soul of my country
As hoes digging their graves drown
the cadence of politicians
singing their wanton dirges of promises

The fluttering feet of infants,
bruised for a pale of water,
beckons to me: I look for

the soul of my country in their steps,
In the faces of hungry children hawking food
I look for it everyday
The soul of my country
In the lives we live
The lies we lie
The deaths we die
The truth we truncate
And i look for the soul of my country
 In the last sigh of Richie Olu Gordon*
Raging like a tsunami to suck the rot in the land
before he ascends to eternity clutching a nation's soul
in the fest of his soul
Richie, are you the soul of my country?

I look for it everyday
The soul of my country
In the dance of the *Sampa*s*;
Mask of *Faluie;**
bow of *Matoma*!*
the stroke of the artist brush
and the lamentation of the poet are you:
the soul of my country?

One day I will stitch the fifty patches of the palette
Into one soul; I'll wear it like *Ashobi**
And dance the Gombay* *for the soul of my country*

Until that day dawns
I will look for it everyday
The soul of my country
In the *sokobana**'s* gong beat
In the tolling church bells and
in the echoes of the azain at dawn.

The soul of my country is silent
A loud thunder has drawn her song
and the smell of her sweat reeks of the toil
on an arid soil, while
despair mounts its kites on their faces

I look for it every day; the soul of my country
I just found it in the penury of its pain.

furrah*-rice flour made to a dough mostly use for sacrifice

Richie Olu Gordon*- a highly respected lecturer and journalist
who made tremendous contribution to nation building
*Sampa*s*;ceremonial dacers
Faluie;*a one arm mask from the mende ethnic
Matoma*a cultural mask from the limba ethnic group
Ashobi*uniforms design to celebrate
Gombay*-local music
sokobana*'s-members of esoteric society

TRIOLOGY

"Man den disgruntle"
"You bobor den dae ya"
" how for do?"
Complete the trilogy of the
 damned of my country;
The prequel of their despair
The sequel of their inertia
And the epilogue of their demise

TEARS

This torrent of tears pouring from the ocean of my soul
Lashing the banks of my eyes
Gathering debris of emotions,
Littering my soul sphere
 and rescinding to the gorge within me
is for those suffering in the outpost of humanity.

Confluence of tears for refugees and orphans of refugee
And refugees of orphans:
A watershed-
 I drown in the vortex of their anguish
 and shed their tears alone in my loneliness
Their tears carved a Nile on my face
My mouth the sea for the river of tears
I chew their tears the salt of their pain embittered me
The anguish of their torment a desert in my soul
The wrinkles on the face of their tired dreams cringing
The insipidness of their dead hopes nauseate me
I swallowed their tears and their tears drowned me
I became a teardrop dripping
Dripping
With a torrent of metaphor
Irrigating the rainforest burnt by the flame of their tears
The Rokel of my soul is flooding
Now I am condemned to write the tale of their tear drops
flooding the land
the tears of the lady of the night at Paddy's
selling pleasure in bowls of sorrow
The tears of Soriebah the fisher man returning home to ailing
wife

leaving behind fishing net stuck to a Korean trawler
The tears of Barome gang raped and tongue raped for being
raped
The tears of Jane yielding to the professor to make the mark
All their tears to a teardrop for posterity to hear their cry
To smell their tears
To feel the fire of their undreamt dreams
To taste the bitterness of their tears
This surge of tears drowning me
Is the tears of the pain of humanity seeking vent
In the eye lids of my verse

I LISTEN

I listen to the sound of silence
 cascading on the ridges of their souls
Like dew on a pond of lilies
I listen to the twang as the veins of their nape snap
 From the weight of a world crouching on their shoulders
I listen to their spirit scampering to sit on the world
I listen to the implosion within their soul
I listen to the thrumming of their spirit
I listen to the stamping of feet as they run life's race
I listen to the faltering steps as they retreat from life's race
I listen to the butterflies flapping wings in the rose gardens of
their souls
I listen to the wind whistling solo song like a forlorn flute
I listen to their dreams spluttering on arid land of reality
I listen to love roaming acres of need dreaming of true love
I listen to the beats between their heart beats
I listen to the crescendo of their cries muffled in sighs
I listen to the platter of tears dripping in the amazons of their
souls
I listen to the cadence of the sounds of our land
I listen to the cacophony of their agony screaming in their eyes
I listen to screeching of the mind of poets like nib on paper
Recording the symphony of silence
I listen to myself listening to all the sounds
Melting into a symphony of eulogies
I listen to my wish for a ballad to drown the eulogies
I listen to the sounds of smiles ripping the frown on their faces
With the jaws of the drums of the harvest season
I listen to their sighs surfing the rice fields
I listen to their thoughts gliding the glades of their soul
I listen like a poet to capture the essence of their existence
I listen and I listen

GAZA STRIP

I stood in the streets of the Gaza Strip
 balancing the memories of Sobibor camp
In   the paradox of the Gaza Strip
I am trapped and stringed to the memories of Auswitch.
On that strip of land strewn with the burden of Buchenwald
Camp
 I held a shriveled wreath
 Waiting to remember the victims of human folly again
I held a never again epitaph to replace yesterday's never again
And my today's never again to be replaced by tomorrow's
never again
In the strip between Hebron and Gaza
I saw humanity yearning for a day without Gaza
And a memory without Sobibor
Yet trapped in a never again circle of demise

WHEN POETS CRY

"Of all the things you took away from me
Just return my handkerchief
Since you left my river
Has never stopped flowing
And I still have the wound
You left in my badge of courage"

- Gbanabom Hallowell

When poets cry the loss of a handkerchief
  their tears are immortalized in verses
Their pain a pyramid
 Defying the wrath of the sun
Their torment an obelisk
For all to feel
What they felt
When the handkerchief was taken away
And for the wound, they gave one to every one
For all of eternity

YOU CAME BACK

You came back
Since you left two decades ago
You became the unsung song in my life
The unwritten lyrics of my soul
The poem between the lines of my poems
The metaphor maiming other metaphors
You came back
Since you left for another world
You became the unseen world of my world
The motif of my unpainted canvas
The note between the notes of my ballad
The artefact capturing a moment lost to the world

You came back
Since you left two decades ago
You became my goldfield unexploited
My unblemished diamond
My treasure trove undiscovered
My green acres unploughed

You came back
Since you left decades ago
 I became an open cage
Sometimes a broken soul
Sometimes an open sore;
Bleeding waiting for your healing
Sometimes a broken winged bird limping
Across the sky to reach you in the other shores

Then the silence
The rumours, the gossips
Then again the silence wrapped in silence

The gossips, the rumours
Then the silence, the silence,
And the deafening silence
Then you came back;
I became an open tomb of hurt;
Hurting for what my youth did to us
I know you hurt because
The seed of your hurt is
 in the trenches of my soul
deep in the heap of my memory

You came back
But you are so far gone
And I am so far away
Yet I embrace you
And my memories
Embrace your memory
We stood still

You came back
And our memories walk our memory lanes
Crossing paths on the cross roads of our youth
You came back
And your smile
Was like the smile you had years ago
And the eyes pierced my soul
Bringing memories of loss
And the lust of my youth
I wish you had stayed
the hurt of your return
Unpeeled the hurt
I wish you had stayed
And I would have remained
a cage locked within itself

an open sore
an open tomb
A broken winged bird
Limping across the sky of familiar hurt
I wish you had stayed
But you came back
Putting my past in my future
You came back.

POEMS FROM SALUTE TO THE REMAINS OF A PEASANT

THE CRY

Rage
Despair
Anguish
Pain
Congealed in the chambers of her soul
As she writhes in the holes of Bunce Island

From the torment of her soul
To the pain of her ovaries
A cry of anguish was born

The cry sucks strength
From the gall of her despair
Ebbs through the tides
Strikes her vocal cords
And explodes into the air
Drenching the cacophony of groans

The Girl slave pants
Like a mother in labor
In the slave house
Where the rape of her humanity
Gave birth to the cry
Her cry mingles
With cries of yesterday
Conspires with sand storm

To torment desert Arabs
The cry drifts in the wind
Unleashing storms
Across oceans

Lashing volcanoes
Takes a sigh in play grounds
Before charging to theRuffian killing fields

The girl perished
The cry survives her mortality
Hers the Eve of cries
The cry of a century
Drilled though the ears of a poet
The poet packages:
The torment, the pain, and the cry
The cry a verse
The verse a poem
A poem of pain

The girl who cried
Died long ago
In the Middle Passage
Survived by a cry
Perhaps she was born
 For just this cry
And the poet
For just this poem

THE WOMAN WHO DANCED

A bundle of hope, a baggage of despair
Braves the cultural Babel and assaults the stage
Shuffling her age and surfing her soul
For the drifting soul of her ancestry in Afro beats.
She wriggles and writhes through the ring of rhythm
Scarred like the sole of her soul.

Alone in the crowded stage of Zanzibar
She danced for the African woman
Trapped in the corn fields of Africa
Suckling and sucking
She danced for the African woman shackled
In the shambles of western glamour
For whom the drum beats no more.

Her contours contract to the rhythm
And rhythm conjure her contours
Unifying her spirit to the ancestral soul
Oozing from the African drums
Her feet pour on the stage like libation
For the ancestor who died for the survival
Of Seigureh and drums in Carnegie Hall.

Decibel after decibel of her heritage
Congealed in melody drill through her ears
Prick her neurons and stimulate her sinews
The woman danced for a generation of women
Who labored and died without a song
Without a dance

STONE BREAKERS

1

A stone on a rock
A hammer sinewed on her trunk
Dreams wedged between rocks
Discordant melody of crushed rocks
Make an orchestra of agony
For the soul of the stone breaker

Piles of broken stones
Rubbles of shattered hopes
Debris of differed dreams
Piled at her feet
Every crushed stone
Is a mile without a milestone
She sits on a rock
 Crushing stones with a hammer
As the sun drench away
The morning years of her life

Her stones build castles
But she sleeps with cattle
Dreaming of those castle
Built with her toil

11

In the break of dawn,
the stone breakers
Of broken hill
 break their sleep; to break stones
 for a breakeven.

After a broken day,
with broken stones
On a broken land
with a broken hammer
and broken hope.
Broken spirit!
Without a break through
They break up to broken homes
awaiting the break of a breakdown

MY POEM IN YOUR POEM

I see my poem in your poem
Dangling in gaps of metaphors
Tiptoeing to scold fleeing images
My verses in the shadow of your verse
Stanzas standing in the starkness of words
Stocking the birth of my poem

I feel the pulse of my poem
Pulsating in your poem
Pumping poesy in my poem
I feel the heart beat of your poem
Pounding in sync with my poem's heart

I hear the muffled voice of my poem
Murmuring like a passing note
And a medley of voices of poets
Of generations past hauling metaphors
To my poem as I read your poem

I feel the feeling of my poem
In every pores of your poem
Filtering a feeling in my poem
Like the feeling in your poem
I sense the spirit of your poem
Caressing the soul of my poem

Now I want to write a poem
With shadows of interlocking cycles
Padded by footprint on the sand
And shell shock children playing in bunkers
Just like the metaphor in your poem

 I see my poem in your poem
And I want to write a poem
Just like your poem
Inspiring poets reading my poem
To write a poem just like my poem
Yet crouching in the womb of your poem

WHEN MY PEN POURS POETRY

When my pen pours poetry
It spurs my pulse to pour
The passion of my soul
To make ink for my pen

When my nib strikes the
Paper, it leaves scars of devastations
In the heart of the paper
For posterity to see

When my pen pours poetry
It crushes the gates of my
Heart and lets out my
Pain for the
Monsters that munch
The mutton and leave
The bones for the mongrels

When my pen pours poetry
It tramples on the minefields
Of my mind and mark me
For a mission

When my pen pours poetry
It pours it for a social change.

HE DID NOT DIE THAT DAY

When the tale of the toll
Of the war was told
In the warmth of our room
My husband folded the sleeves of his Ronko
Sharpened his spear
Smeared mafoi on his body
Beat his chest
Spewed honey bees
The lion growled;
"I will die for your honor"

When the renegade came
 Violence galore;
Looting my honor
Raping my dignity
Entombing my womb
He did not die that day
His heart pounds
Stomach of beehive rumbles
His Ronko and spear
 Behind the door
Next to the bottle of Mafoi
Remained untouched
He shriek under the bed
  As the renegades killed my honor
But he did not die that day
Yet he is dying everyday
 For not dying that day

Ronko –Traditional cloth made of rough cotton and imbibed
with charms to protect the owner

MAFOI-A themne people word for a concoction of herbs with healing and protective powers used by traditional warriors

HE DIED THAT DAY

When the tale of the toll
Of the war was trumpeted in our quarters
My husband grabbed his gun donned his fatigues
Kissed our two and half children good bye
The lion in him growled; *"I will die for your honour"*
He jumped in the truck singing war songs
He met the rebels in the fields of Bomaru
He fired his gun for my honour
He killed for our sovereignty
Yet he was out manoeuvred; his gun fluttered
And his platoon petered

Yet my man kept his oath
And died that day for my honour

He lives everyday
Because he died that day

I WANT TO CRY

I want to cry
A cry of pain
Panting in perils
Painted like paradise

I want to cry
A cry of anguish
Anchoring pent up anger
For the devil Angels
Robbing and raping humanity

I want to cry
A cry of solitude
Felt in the servitude
Of the Mongols
I want to cry
A cry of agony
For the trivialities
Spun to give credit
To the futility of life

I want to cry
A hallow and harrowing cry
For the hollowness
Of wallowing in a hollow world
I want to cry
A shattering cry
Shaking the shackles
Of a shambled world

DREAMS

(DEDICATED TO TUDADU JARIA SESAY)
Don't let go your dream,
Cling to it, like a mother
In a war ravaged land
will cling to a dying child.

Don't let go your dream
Clutch at it, like a drowning
Man will do to a straw

Don't let go your dream
Embrace it, like a love
Starved Romeo will do to a Juliet.

Don't let go your dream
Suck it like a breast starved
Child will to her mother's nipple.

Don't let go your dream
Cling, clutch, embrace and suck
Till you perish of flourish with it.
Don't let go you dream.

LET ME

For years I frolicked in folly
Fending for frailties on the fringes
Shunning your warmth
Today I return like a prodigal poet
Pouncing at your door to let me muse once more
Shoot missiles of metaphors
Bombs of similes
To shatter into shambles
The shackles on the minds of renegades
Contenting in our discontent
Wedge my nib in their loins
Like the bayonet on innocence's loins
Ripping their entrails for vultures to dine
Steer at the streak of guilt in their eyes
As they beg for death on the gallows
of Pademba Prison
Write about the wrath writhing
inside me like a scorched serpent
For the wretched wreaking havoc
On my mother land
Pour the pulsating pain
In my country's pulse
As she dies of overdose of greed
Rage like a hurricane
Burning to ashes looters
Looting the vaults of my country

SALUTE TO THE REMAINS OF A PEASANT

From a thatched hut of mud
On the fringes of the forest
To an unmarked heap of mud
In the depth of the forest
His mortal mould of mud
Is laid to rest
After a life of unrest in the mud

MY WILL

When I die bury
Me deep in the
Bowls of the earth

Place granite stones on my coffin
Erect your monuments of filth for epitaph.
Or
Cremate my body, sprinkle
The ashes into the sea
Or
Grind the remains of
My mortal mould and
Feed your pigs and soil
Or
Hang my remains on
The cotton tree for
Vultures and flies to feed on
Or
Dissect me and preserve
My entrails and skeleton
In the laboratory
Mark them specimen A and B.
But when I die,
Don't bury my poetry
In the prison of your
Shelves under your beds
In your cockroach
Infested boxes for mice

And cockroaches to dine
Don't pluck the pages of
My poetry to wrap crumbs

Read my poetry
Sing my poetry
Act my poetry
The only legacy
I will leave
To the cruel world

I WRITE WHAT I FEEL

No one feels the pangs
Of a mother in labor
But the mother in labor

No one feels the grip
Of the hangman's rope
But the hanged man

No one feels the strains
Of mending soles
But the mender of soles

No one feels the burden
Of a luggage

But the carrier of the luggage

No one feels the nagging
The throbbing, the probing,
The gnawing, the curiosity
The anxiety on the
Mind of the writer
But the writer

No one feels what I write
No one tells me what I write
I write what I feel.

AT TELLU BONGOR

Dedicated to the 63 people massacred by RUF rebels at Tellu Bongor

What
Prowls like a hungry tiger in the Gola forest of my mind
 Is rage nursed to puncture your heart for raping your mother at Tellu Bongor.

What
Rages like a rabied dog in the dustbin of my mind is rebellion, against you for butchering you father at Tellu Bongor

What
Fires like a hurricane in the savanna of my mind is disdain for you for entombing the wombs at Tellu Bongor.
Nutured by pain
Termites gnaw the walls of my mind
And the blisters on my hands, red like the intifadas in the Gaza Strip
Burn from touching the limbs that you dismembered at Tellu Bongor
And a hungry lion in the kailahun of my mind is enraged
To snatch your galled heart at Tellu Bongor

NO

(On a commission to write poem of love)

No I cannot write it here
That poem that will
Scoop the mind-fields of
Mindless warmongers
Munching souls of mortals like
A monster, for muddled up cause.

No I cannot write it here
That poem that will diffuse
Nuclear bombs, stop arms escalation
Knock of scud weapons like
Patriot missile.

No I cannot write it here
That poem that will clean
Hate ridden hearts with a
Love that has no
Color, creed and race.

No I cannot write it here
That poem that will be poor
In verse but rich in love
For all of God's creation

No I cannot write it here
Those poetry children portray
In playgrounds, birds sing in shrubs.

No I can not write it,
But I want you to read it

In the childhood anthology
It is there, the poetry of love
That brought us here.

I can see it in that child
Feel it in her smiles
Sense it in her chemistry
Hear it in her breath.

Yet I refuse to write it
But I want you to read it
Read the rhyme scheme
In the rhythmic movement of
Their feet in the playground.

Read the similes in their
Smiles, and the metaphor
In their mood.

Read it, it is there
The poetry of love
But I cannot write it.

ONCE AGAIN

This wound in the Earth
Is the grave of my heart
I traverse a landscape stripped of its own heart
In search of hope

A scar in the Earth
Marks the grave of my soul
I roam with a soulless
Body searching for my soul
In the womb of the earth, My life is a compass
 drifting like driftwood
In turbulent waters

A site on the vast Earth
Blurs my sight
I grope in dens and graves
Without a sight
For Oumou Kultum Sesay
Buried in the earth's womb
And search for her likes
To mother me once again

IN-DEPENDENCE

She came drench in a bloody placenta
With an uncut cord
Gasping midwives who performed
The liberation caesarean without
Anesthetics in an open theatre
Gazed at the enigma:
The dumb lumps named
The free but chained
The Independent but dependent
The aged but young
The weaned but suckling
The born but unborn
I-N-D-E-P-E-N-D-E-N-C-E

Printed in the United States
By Bookmasters